Y0-AGJ-604

A **BoomerView**™ ElderCare Guide

Tracking Your Medicine

How to Keep It Simple and Safe

This Guide belongs to:

_____
Name

_____
Phone Number

Tracking Your Medicine

How to Keep It Simple and Safe

Laurel Zien, M.A.

BoomerView Press
El Cerrito, California
www.**BoomerView**.com

Published by **BoomerView Press** in the **BoomerView** *ElderCare Guide Series.*

BoomerView, BoomerView Press, BoomerView.com, and the BoomerView logo, consisting of a heart under a magnifying glass, are trademarks of **BoomerView Press.**

ISBN 0-9741331-0-8

Manufactured in the United States of America.
10 9 8 7 6 5 4 3 2

Cover Design by George Foster. www.fostercovers.com
Interior Design & Typography by Pete Masterson, Aeonix Publishing Group. www.aeonix.com

Attention Corporations, Health and Professional Organizations, and Non-Profit Associations: Quantity discounts are available on bulk purchases of this Guide for educational or fund-raising purposes. Special guides can also be created to meet specific needs. For information, please contact: **BoomerView Press,** 3020 El Cerrito Plaza #376, El Cerrito, CA 94530, or sales@BoomerView.com.

The following stories are unidentified to respect the privacy of the individuals and families who shared them.

"I opened the kitchen cupboard, and it was crammed full of prescription bottles. Many were expired, but the bottles were almost full. About ten had recent dates, but I had no idea which ones my mother was taking now or what the pills were for. There were four different doctors on the labels and no phone numbers to call. It was frightening, and I didn't know where to begin."

"My dad had fallen and was hospitalized with a broken hip. He knew he was taking pills for gout and high blood pressure. But his medicine cabinet had six other prescriptions as well, and we didn't know which ones he took. His pain medication was making him confused, and it was nearly a week before we got all of his pills back on track. We were lucky nothing serious happened."

"Dad was suffering from late-life depression and anxiety. His diabetes and thyroid problems also added to the list of drugs he took daily. We lived across the country, and when he got pneumonia, we were lost. We didn't know who his doctors were, which drugs he was taking or how often. Putting together his list of medicines for the hospital was a real challenge and took so long that he did go into withdrawal. I wish we'd gotten the information together sooner."

"The average older person is taking more than four prescription medications at once plus two over-the-counter medications. Up to 50% of those who use medicines do not use them as directed. To guard against potential problems with drugs, older adults must be knowledgeable about what they take and how it makes them feel."   —*U.S. Food and Drug Administration*

"Every year, non-compliance with drug treatment causes an estimated 125,000 deaths from cardiovascular disease... up to 23% of nursing home admissions and 10% of hospital admissions."
—*Office of the U.S. Inspector General*

❖

Most of the information in this Guide is generally available, replicated in numerous sources, and is in the public domain. Among the sources of information consulted, but not directly quoted: National Institutes of Health/National Institute on Aging; U.S. Food and Drug Administration; National Council on Patient Information and Education; National Council on the Aging; and the Agency for Healthcare Policy and Research of the Department of Health and Human Services.

Contents

Important Caution to the Reader

This publication is meant to be used as an aid to keeping track of medications. It is designed and intended to be used only by alert, attentive, and competent individuals. Special caution must be taken by individuals — and caregivers of individuals — who are not themselves capable of using this publication properly, whether due to age, infirmity, or any other physical, mental, or emotional factors.

This publication is meant to be used under the advice and direction of medical professionals who are familiar with all of the medications that are being tracked. Readers are strongly encouraged to show this publication to all prescribing and treating physicians and other medical professionals in order to secure their approval and guidance for the proper use of this publication.

This publication does not take the place of medical advice, supervision, and care and should not be used as a substitute for obtaining such services from qualified practitioners. Neither the author nor the publisher is rendering medical advice or otherwise rendering medical services. As noted above, readers should consult an appropriate medical professional in conjunction with using or relying on any of the advice, information or other contents of this publication.

This book is published, distributed, and sold without warranties or guarantees of any kind, express or implied, and the author and publisher disclaim any responsibility or liability for any loss, damage, or other consequences resulting directly or indirectly from any use of this publication or the information, advice or other contents of this publication.

Introduction

The stories are likely familiar. We drop in unexpectedly and watch a parent struggle with daily tasks. Or perhaps your partner falls or has a stroke. An older person's health can change quickly, and, seemingly overnight, everything is a challenge. Whether we live far away or across the street, as adult children of aging parents or as a friend or partner, we step in to help. We need information—on their medicines, health and home care, assistive devices, and housing, and we need it fast. We also need it simple.

This first **BoomerView**™ Eldercare Guide, *Tracking Your Medicine: How to Keep It Simple and Safe,* addresses one major challenge: dealing with multiple medicines. The Guide is designed for use by anyone taking more than a daily vitamin, including baby boomers, seniors, adult children of aging parents, and caregivers. It has simple, short forms to give us and our loved ones peace of mind and our doctors the information they need to provide the best care possible.

Many people struggle to manage multiple medicines prescribed by as many as five physicians. These specialists often are unaware of the full catalogue of drugs (including over-the-counter items) we use. Although it would be wonderful if one doctor were in charge of coordinating our care, this rarely happens. Sometimes we are told to stop taking a drug prescribed by another physician. Sometimes we take two drugs with different names but with similar ingredients and purposes which may cause over-medication.

The average senior takes several drugs every day. When an illness occurs and new medicines are added to the mix, the opportunities for confusion or non-compliance increase. Prescriptions may be effectively tracked by modern computer systems while we're in the hospital or by our regular pharmacy if we have one. But we still have to figure it all out and keep it straight once we get home. Then we wonder what "take as directed" means or if we are supposed to take that pill with or without food. Rarely do we understand what a drug does, how long it takes to work, or if it's safe for us.

We are fortunate to have medicines which add comfort and perhaps years to our life, and we all think we have them under control. Yet when illness or an emergency occurs, we may suffer with inadequate pain management, depression, memory and sleep loss, drug-induced confusion, temporary hallucinations, or anxiety.

Thousands of hospital and nursing home admissions annually are the result of difficulties in following prescribed medicine treatment plans, side effects from medications, serious drug interactions, or duplication of prescription and/or over-the-counter medicines.

We need better communication with our doctors and pharmacists and a clear, basic understanding of the medicines we take and how to use them. We need to ask questions and get answers about our prescriptions and over-the-counter drugs, how they interact, and how they affect an aging body.

Tracking Your Medicine: How to Keep It Simple and Safe can improve the success of your medical treatments and help avoid dangerous drug interactions if you use it and keep it up-to-date. Help your doctors help you. Don't let your pills—or not taking your pills—make you sick.

This Guide is designed and intended to be used only by alert, attentive, and competent individuals. Special caution must be taken by individuals—and caregivers—who are not themselves capable of using this Guide properly, whether due to age, infirmity, or any other physical, mental, or emotional factors.

How To Use *Tracking Your Medicine*

1. Fill out the forms. It's easy and won't take long.

   ✦ The PillTracker Form is a guide to help you ask your doctor about your new or current prescriptions. Also use it to ask the druggist for additional information when you pick up medicines from the pharmacy. Fill out a separate PillTracker Form for each prescription medicine you are now taking with as much information as you know about that medicine. This will clarify the instructions for you. Fill out a new form every time you get a new prescription.

   ✦ The Medicine List is the place to record *all* prescriptions, over-the-counter medicines, vitamins, and herbal and homeopathic remedies you currently are taking. Update the List whenever you add new medicines or change doses or amounts. Include everything listed on your PillTracker Forms.

   ✦ The brief Medical History section records your current medical conditions and allergies and can be reviewed by your practitioner or used by emergency healthcare personnel.

   ✦ A Medicine Schedule will help you organize pill taking times and directions. Select and fill out a Schedule that works for you, or use it as a model to make your own.

   ✦ The Phone Book section centralizes your medical and emergency contact numbers.

   ✦ The Resources Section has Web sites to help you find additional drug information.

   ✦ The 34 Vital Tips on Medicines are surprising, and they will help keep you on track.

Then…

2. Every time you visit your doctor or pharmacy, take the Guide with you and

   ✦ Have the doctor or pharmacist review your PillTracker Forms and check for potential drug interactions by reviewing your Medicine List and Schedule.

   ✦ Have him/her complete the individual PillTracker Forms for your current prescriptions if you are missing information.

   ✦ When you get a new prescription, fill out the PillTracker Form right away with the doctor or pharmacist. Ask the questions! Take notes! Remember, add it to your Medicine List and Schedule.

3. If you go to the hospital, **take this Guide with you** so your doctors know all your current medicines and other remedies.

That's all there is to it. Don't wait. Don't wish you'd done it sooner. Start tracking your medicines now. You, your loved ones, and your doctors will be glad you did.

Here's to your good health!

❖

The **PillTracker Form**

On the next page is a PillTracker Form filled out with sample information, followed by a number of blank forms for your use. Gather your current prescriptions together, and fill out a form for each medicine you currently take. If there is something you don't know and it's not on the label, leave the space blank. You can get the information from your pharmacist or doctor on your next visit. Remember, filling out the forms helps clarify the correct directions for each pill. The bottom line is to take your medicines as prescribed.

❖

PillTracker Form (Sample)

Dr. Smith

Pharmacy Super D

1. Name of the drug ___Prescription A___

Dosage ___25___ mg. Color ___white___ Shape ___round___

2. What is it for? ___headache___

How long do I take it? ___30 days___

3. When do I take it? ___4___ times a day.   Every ___4___ hours.   (check box) ☐ AM or ☐ PM.

How many pills each time? ___1___   Maximum pills/doses per day ___4___.

Do NOT take with ___grapefruit or grapefruit juice___.

Take with: ☐ food ☐ milk ☒ water ☐ juice ☐ coffee ☐ tea   Take ☐ before / ☐ after meals? (ck box)

Can the pills be cut? ☒ yes ☐ no   Can the pills be crushed? ☐ yes ☒ no   (check box)

4. How long before it works? ___1 day___   How do I know it's working? ___headache gone___

5. What are common side effects/warnings? ___stomach cramps___   ___vomiting___

I should call your office if I experience what side effects? ___vomiting___

6. What if I miss a dose? ___wait until the next dose___

Date Started ___4/30___   Date Stopped _____   Observations: ☒ Effective ☐ Not Effective (ck box)

My notes: ___gave me dry mouth but worked pretty well___

PillTracker Form

Dr. _____   Pharmacy _____

1. Name of the drug _____ Dosage _____ mg. Color _____ Shape _____

2. What is it for? _____ How long do I take it? _____

3. When do I take it? _____ times a day.   Every _____ hours.   (check box) ☐ AM or ☐ PM.

   How many pills each time? _____   Maximum pills/doses per day _____ .

   Do NOT take with _____ .

   Take with: ☐ food ☐ milk ☐ water ☐ juice ☐ coffee ☐ tea Take ☐ before / ☐ after meals? (ck box)

   Can the pills be cut? ☐ yes ☐ no   Can the pills be crushed? ☐ yes ☐ no   (check box)

4. How long before it works? _____ How do I know it's working? _____

5. What are common side effects/warnings? _____

   I should call your office if I experience what side effects? _____

6. What if I miss a dose? _____

Date Started _____ Date Stopped _____ Observations: ☐ Effective ☐ Not Effective (ck box)

My notes: _____

PillTracker Form

Dr. _____

Pharmacy _____

1. Name of the drug _____ Dosage _____ mg. Color _____ Shape _____

2. What is it for? _____ How long do I take it? _____

3. When do I take it? _____ times a day. Every _____ hours. (check box) ☐ AM or ☐ PM.

How many pills each time? _____ Maximum pills/doses per day _____.

Do NOT take with _____.

Take with: ☐ food ☐ milk ☐ water ☐ juice ☐ coffee ☐ tea Take ☐ before / ☐ after meals? (ck box)

Can the pills be cut? ☐ yes ☐ no   Can the pills be crushed? ☐ yes ☐ no   (check box)

4. How long before it works? _____ How do I know it's working? _____

5. What are common side effects/warnings? _____

I should call your office if I experience what side effects? _____

6. What if I miss a dose? _____

Date Started _____ Date Stopped _____ Observations: ☐ Effective ☐ Not Effective (ck box)

My notes: _____

PillTracker Form

Dr. _____

Pharmacy _____

1. Name of the drug _____ Dosage _____ mg. Color _____ Shape _____

2. What is it for? _____

   How long do I take it? _____

3. When do I take it? _____ times a day. Every _____ hours. (check box) ☐ AM or ☐ PM.

   How many pills each time? _____ Maximum pills/doses per day _____ .

   Do NOT take with _____ .

   Take with: ☐ food ☐ milk ☐ water ☐ juice ☐ coffee ☐ tea Take ☐ before / ☐ after meals? (ck box)

   Can the pills be cut? ☐ yes ☐ no   Can the pills be crushed? ☐ yes ☐ no   (check box)

4. How long before it works? _____ How do I know it's working? _____

5. What are common side effects/warnings? _____

   I should call your office if I experience what side effects? _____

6. What if I miss a dose? _____

Date Started _____ Date Stopped _____ Observations: ☐ Effective ☐ Not Effective (ck box)

My notes: _____

PillTracker Form

Dr. _____ Pharmacy _____

1. Name of the drug _____ Dosage _____ mg. Color _____ Shape _____

2. What is it for? _____ How long do I take it? _____

3. When do I take it? _____ times a day. Every _____ hours. (check box) ☐ AM or ☐ PM.

    How many pills each time? _____ Maximum pills/doses per day _____.

    Do NOT take with _____.

    Take with: ☐ food ☐ milk ☐ water ☐ juice ☐ coffee ☐ tea Take ☐ before / ☐ after meals? (ck box)

    Can the pills be cut? ☐ yes ☐ no   Can the pills be crushed? ☐ yes ☐ no (check box)

4. How long before it works? _____ How do I know it's working? _____

5. What are common side effects/warnings? _____

    I should call your office if I experience what side effects? _____

6. What if I miss a dose? _____

Date Started _____ Date Stopped _____ Observations: ☐ Effective ☐ Not Effective (ck box)

My notes: _____

PillTracker Form

Dr. _____   Pharmacy _____

1. Name of the drug _____ Dosage _____ mg. Color _____ Shape _____

2. What is it for? _____ How long do I take it? _____

3. When do I take it? _____ times a day.   Every _____ hours. (check box) ☐ AM or ☐ PM.

   How many pills each time? _____   Maximum pills/doses per day _____ .

   Do NOT take with _____ .

   Take with: ☐ food ☐ milk ☐ water ☐ juice ☐ coffee ☐ tea Take ☐ before / ☐ after meals? (ck box)

   Can the pills be cut? ☐ yes ☐ no   Can the pills be crushed? ☐ yes ☐ no   (check box)

4. How long before it works? _____ How do I know it's working? _____

5. What are common side effects/warnings? _____

   I should call your office if I experience what side effects? _____

6. What if I miss a dose? _____

Date Started _____ Date Stopped _____ Observations: ☐ Effective ☐ Not Effective (ck box)

My notes: _____

PillTracker Form

Dr. _____ Pharmacy _____

1. Name of the drug _____ Dosage _____ mg. Color _____ Shape _____

2. What is it for? _____ How long do I take it? _____

3. When do I take it? _____ times a day. Every _____ hours. (check box) ☐ AM or ☐ PM.

   How many pills each time? _____ Maximum pills/doses per day _____ .

   Do NOT take with _____ .

   Take with: ☐ food ☐ milk ☐ water ☐ juice ☐ coffee ☐ tea Take ☐ before / ☐ after meals? (ck box)

   Can the pills be cut? ☐ yes ☐ no   Can the pills be crushed? ☐ yes ☐ no   (check box)

4. How long before it works? _____ How do I know it's working? _____

5. What are common side effects/warnings? _____

   I should call your office if I experience what side effects? _____

6. What if I miss a dose? _____

Date Started _____ Date Stopped _____ Observations: ☐ Effective ☐ Not Effective (ck box)

My notes: _____

PillTracker Form

Dr. _____ Pharmacy _____

1. Name of the drug _____ Dosage _____ mg. Color _____ Shape _____

2. What is it for? _____ How long do I take it? _____

3. When do I take it? _____ times a day. Every _____ hours. (check box) ☐ AM or ☐ PM.

   How many pills each time? _____ Maximum pills/doses per day _____.

   Do NOT take with _____.

   Take with: ☐ food ☐ milk ☐ water ☐ juice ☐ coffee ☐ tea Take ☐ before / ☐ after meals? (ck box)

   Can the pills be cut? ☐ yes ☐ no   Can the pills be crushed? ☐ yes ☐ no   (check box)

4. How long before it works? _____ How do I know it's working? _____

5. What are common side effects/warnings? _____

   I should call your office if I experience what side effects? _____

6. What if I miss a dose? _____

Date Started _____ Date Stopped _____ Observations: ☐ Effective ☐ Not Effective (ck box)

My notes: _____

PillTracker Form

Dr. _____ Pharmacy _____

1. Name of the drug _____ Dosage _____ mg. Color _____ Shape _____

2. What is it for? _____ How long do I take it? _____

3. When do I take it? _____ times a day.   Every _____ hours.   (check box) ☐ AM or ☐ PM.

   How many pills each time? _____   Maximum pills/doses per day _____.

   Do NOT take with _____.

   Take with: ☐ food ☐ milk ☐ water ☐ juice ☐ coffee ☐ tea Take ☐ before / ☐ after meals? (ck box)

   Can the pills be cut? ☐ yes ☐ no   Can the pills be crushed? ☐ yes ☐ no   (check box)

4. How long before it works? _____   How do I know it's working? _____

5. What are common side effects/warnings? _____

   I should call your office if I experience what side effects? _____

6. What if I miss a dose? _____

Date Started _____ Date Stopped _____ Observations: ☐ Effective ☐ Not Effective (ck box)

My notes: _____

PillTracker Form

Dr. _____   Pharmacy _____

1. Name of the drug _____ Dosage _____ mg. Color _____ Shape _____

2. What is it for? _____ How long do I take it? _____

3. When do I take it? _____ times a day.   Every _____ hours.   (check box) ☐ AM or ☐ PM.

   How many pills each time? _____   Maximum pills/doses per day _____ .

   Do NOT take with _____ .

   Take with: ☐ food ☐ milk ☐ water ☐ juice ☐ coffee ☐ tea Take ☐ before / ☐ after meals? (ck box)

   Can the pills be cut? ☐ yes ☐ no   Can the pills be crushed? ☐ yes ☐ no   (check box)

4. How long before it works? _____ How do I know it's working? _____

5. What are common side effects/warnings? _____

   I should call your office if I experience what side effects? _____

6. What if I miss a dose? _____

Date Started _____ Date Stopped _____ Observations: ☐ Effective ☐ Not Effective (ck box)

My notes:

PillTracker Form

Dr. _____   Pharmacy _____

1. Name of the drug _____ Dosage _____ mg. Color _____ Shape _____

2. What is it for? _____ How long do I take it? _____

3. When do I take it? _____ times a day.   Every _____ hours.   (check box) ☐ AM or ☐ PM.

   How many pills each time? _____   Maximum pills/doses per day _____ .

   Do NOT take with _____ .

   Take with: ☐ food ☐ milk ☐ water ☐ juice ☐ coffee ☐ tea Take ☐ before / ☐ after meals? (ck box)

   Can the pills be cut? ☐ yes ☐ no   Can the pills be crushed? ☐ yes ☐ no   (check box)

4. How long before it works? _____ How do I know it's working? _____

5. What are common side effects/warnings? _____

   I should call your office if I experience what side effects? _____

6. What if I miss a dose? _____

   Date Started _____ Date Stopped _____   Observations: ☐ Effective ☐ Not Effective (ck box)

   My notes: _____

PillTracker Form

Dr. _____

Pharmacy _____

1. Name of the drug _____ Dosage _____ mg. Color _____ Shape _____

2. What is it for? _____ How long do I take it? _____

3. When do I take it? _____ times a day. Every _____ hours. (check box) ☐ AM or ☐ PM.

How many pills each time? _____ Maximum pills/doses per day _____ .

Do NOT take with _____ .

Take with: ☐ food ☐ milk ☐ water ☐ juice ☐ coffee ☐ tea Take ☐ before / ☐ after meals? (ck box)

Can the pills be cut? ☐ yes ☐ no   Can the pills be crushed? ☐ yes ☐ no   (check box)

4. How long before it works? _____ How do I know it's working? _____

5. What are common side effects/warnings? _____

I should call your office if I experience what side effects? _____

6. What if I miss a dose? _____

Date Started _____ Date Stopped _____ Observations: ☐ Effective ☐ Not Effective (ck box)

My notes: _____

PillTracker Form

Dr. _____   Pharmacy _____

1. Name of the drug _____ Dosage _____ mg. Color _____ Shape _____

2. What is it for? _____ How long do I take it? _____

3. When do I take it? _____ times a day.   Every _____ hours. (check box) ☐ AM or ☐ PM.

   How many pills each time? _____   Maximum pills/doses per day _____.

   Do NOT take with _____.

   Take with: ☐ food ☐ milk ☐ water ☐ juice ☐ coffee ☐ tea Take ☐ before / ☐ after meals? (ck box)

   Can the pills be cut? ☐ yes ☐ no   Can the pills be crushed? ☐ yes ☐ no   (check box)

4. How long before it works? _____   How do I know it's working? _____

5. What are common side effects/warnings? _____

   I should call your office if I experience what side effects? _____

6. What if I miss a dose? _____

Date Started _____   Date Stopped _____   Observations: ☐ Effective ☐ Not Effective (ck box)

My notes:

PillTracker Form

Dr. _____ Pharmacy _____

1. Name of the drug _____ Dosage _____ mg. Color _____ Shape _____

2. What is it for? _____ How long do I take it? _____

3. When do I take it? _____ times a day. Every _____ hours. (check box) ☐ AM or ☐ PM.

   How many pills each time? _____ Maximum pills/doses per day _____ .

   Do NOT take with _____ .

   Take with: ☐ food ☐ milk ☐ water ☐ juice ☐ coffee ☐ tea Take ☐ before / ☐ after meals? (ck box)

   Can the pills be cut? ☐ yes ☐ no   Can the pills be crushed? ☐ yes ☐ no   (check box)

4. How long before it works? _____ How do I know it's working? _____

5. What are common side effects/warnings? _____

   I should call your office if I experience what side effects? _____

6. What if I miss a dose? _____

Date Started _____ Date Stopped _____ Observations: ☐ Effective ☐ Not Effective (ck box)

My notes: _____

27

PillTracker Form

Dr. _____   Pharmacy _____

1. Name of the drug _____ Dosage _____ mg. Color _____ Shape _____

2. What is it for? _____ How long do I take it? _____

3. When do I take it? _____ times a day.   Every _____ hours.   (check box) ☐ AM or ☐ PM.

   How many pills each time? _____   Maximum pills/doses per day _____.

   Do NOT take with _____.

   Take with: ☐ food ☐ milk ☐ water ☐ juice ☐ coffee ☐ tea   Take ☐ before / ☐ after meals? (ck box)

   Can the pills be cut? ☐ yes ☐ no   Can the pills be crushed? ☐ yes ☐ no   (check box)

4. How long before it works? _____ How do I know it's working? _____

5. What are common side effects/warnings? _____

   I should call your office if I experience what side effects? _____

6. What if I miss a dose? _____

Date Started _____ Date Stopped _____ Observations: ☐ Effective ☐ Not Effective (ck box)

My notes: _____

PillTracker Form

Dr. _____

Pharmacy _____

1. Name of the drug _____ Dosage _____ mg. Color _____ Shape _____

2. What is it for? _____

   How long do I take it? _____

3. When do I take it? _____ times a day. Every _____ hours. (check box) ☐ AM or ☐ PM.

   How many pills each time? _____ Maximum pills/doses per day _____ .

   Do NOT take with _____ .

   Take with: ☐ food ☐ milk ☐ water ☐ juice ☐ coffee ☐ tea Take ☐ before / ☐ after meals? (ck box)

   Can the pills be cut? ☐ yes ☐ no   Can the pills be crushed? ☐ yes ☐ no   (check box)

4. How long before it works? _____ How do I know it's working? _____

5. What are common side effects/warnings? _____

   I should call your office if I experience what side effects? _____

6. What if I miss a dose? _____

   Date Started _____ Date Stopped _____ Observations: ☐ Effective ☐ Not Effective (ck box)

   My notes: _____

PillTracker Form

Dr. _____

1. Name of the drug _____ Pharmacy _____ Dosage _____ mg. Color _____ Shape _____

2. What is it for? _____ How long do I take it? _____

3. When do I take it? _____ times a day. Every _____ hours. (check box) ☐ AM or ☐ PM.

   How many pills each time? _____ Maximum pills/doses per day _____.

   Do NOT take with _____.

   Take with: ☐ food ☐ milk ☐ water ☐ juice ☐ coffee ☐ tea Take ☐ before / ☐ after meals? (ck box)

   Can the pills be cut? ☐ yes ☐ no   Can the pills be crushed? ☐ yes ☐ no (check box)

4. How long before it works? _____ How do I know it's working? _____

5. What are common side effects/warnings? _____

   I should call your office if I experience what side effects? _____

6. What if I miss a dose? _____

Date Started _____ Date Stopped _____ Observations: ☐ Effective ☐ Not Effective (ck box)

My notes: _____

PillTracker Form

Dr. _____   Pharmacy _____

1. Name of the drug _____ Dosage _____ mg. Color _____ Shape _____

2. What is it for? _____ How long do I take it? _____

3. When do I take it? _____ times a day.   Every _____ hours. (check box) ☐ AM or ☐ PM.

   How many pills each time? _____ Maximum pills/doses per day _____ .

   Do NOT take with _____ .

   Take with: ☐ food ☐ milk ☐ water ☐ juice ☐ coffee ☐ tea Take ☐ before / ☐ after meals? (ck box)

   Can the pills be cut? ☐ yes ☐ no   Can the pills be crushed? ☐ yes ☐ no   (check box)

4. How long before it works? _____ How do I know it's working? _____

5. What are common side effects/warnings? _____

   I should call your office if I experience what side effects? _____

6. What if I miss a dose? _____

Date Started _____ Date Stopped _____ Observations: ☐ Effective ☐ Not Effective (ck box)

My notes: _____

31

The Medicine List (Sample Page)

See the chart below for a good way to fill out the Medicine List. Blank forms are on following pages. Be sure to include all your current prescriptions and the names of all of your over-the-counter (OTC) medicines, vitamins, herbal or homeopathic remedies, and other supplements. Don't forget to include antacids, nose sprays, allergy pills, inhalers, eye drops, ointments, or creams you use. When you begin a new prescription or other new medicine of any kind or change doses, be sure to add it to the List. When you stop a medicine, draw a line through it and add the stop date.

Name of Medicine	Dose	Timing	Start Date	Reason for Taking, Comments, and Stop Date
Aspirin	81mg	daily	2000	heart
Multi-Vitamin	1	daily	1999	general health
Prescription A	150mg	2 x day	12/02	gastritis
Night-time cold medicine	spoon	p.m.	2/03	bad cold --stopped 3/22/03
Prescription B	500mg	3 x day	3/03	diabetes
Prescription C	20mg	1 x day	3/03	depression - take w/food
Eye Drops	2 drops	2 x day	2001	dry, itchy eyes

Medicine List

Name of Medicine	Dose	Timing	Start Date	Reason for Taking, Comments, and Stop Date

Medicine List

Name of Medicine	Dose	Timing	Start Date	Reason for Taking, Comments, and Stop Date

Medicine List

Medicine List

Name of Medicine	Dose	Timing	Start Date	Reason for Taking, Comments, and Stop Date

Medicine List

Medicine List

Name of Medicine	Dose	Timing	Start Date	Reason for Taking, Comments, and Stop Date

Short Medical History Form

This information is very important in an emergency and for your medical practitioners to know.

Name	Date of Birth	
Primary Dr.	Insurance Co.	Policy Number
Blood Type	Insurance Phone	

Medical Conditions: (check box)

☐ Diabetes ☐ Depression ☐ Heart Disease ☐ Stroke
☐ Asthma ☐ Ulcer ☐ Cancer ☐ High Blood pressure
☐ Anemia ☐ Liver Disease ☐ Arthritis ☐ Chronic Lung Disease
☐ Kidney Disease ☐ Glaucoma

Other Conditions: (Specify)

Allergies to Medicines or Substances: (Specify)

Do you wear: (check box) ☐ Medical Implants ☐ Pacemaker ☐ Dentures
☐ Contact Lenses ☐ Glasses ☐ Artificial Limbs ☐ Hearing Aid

Other Medical Problems:

Social Drugs Used: (check box)
☐ Alcohol ☐ Caffeine ☐ Tobacco

Medical History

Medicine Schedules

There are two types of schedules presented here, each followed by a set of blank forms. Choose the form you prefer, and use pencil, as medicines and doses change frequently. Feel free to modify the forms, or design your own using one of these as a model. If you make a copy, you can post it where you can see it as a reminder.

Medicine Schedule A (Sample)

Name	How many to take	How to take it	Times of day you take medication – Note if you take the medicine before, with, or after meals.			
			Morning	Noon	Dinner	Bedtime
Prescription A	1	with O.j.	8 A.M.			Bedtime
Prescription B	1 1/2	with food	breakfast	Lunch	dinner	
Prescription C	1/2	empty stomach		Before Lunch		
Aspirin	1	with food	breakfast			
Vitamin	1	with food	breakfast			

Medicine Schedule A

Name	How many to take	How to take it	Times of day you take medication – Note if you take the medicine before, with, or after meals.			
			Morning	Noon	Dinner	Bedtime

Medicine Schedule

Medicine Schedule A

Name	How many to take	How to take it	Times of day you take medication – Note if you take the medicine before, with, or after meals.			
			Morning	Noon	Dinner	Bedtime

Medicine Schedule

Medicine Schedule A

Name	How many to take	How to take it	Times of day you take medication – Note if you take the medicine before, with, or after meals.			
			Morning	Noon	Dinner	Bedtime

Medicine Schedule B (Sample)

	Sun	Mon	Tue	Wed	Thur	Fri	Sat
Morning	Vitamin* Presc. A* Aspirin*	Vitamin* Presc. A* Aspirin*	Vitamin* Presc. A* Aspirin*	Vitamin* Presc. A* Aspirin*	Vitamin* Presc. A* Aspirin*	Vitamin* Presc. A* Aspirin*	Vitamin* Presc. A* Aspirin*
Lunchtime	Presc. B*	Presc. B*	Presc. B*	Presc. B*	Presc. B*	Presc. B*	Presc. B*
Dinner-time	Presc. C Empty stomach	Presc. C Empty stomach	Presc. C Empty stomach	Presc. C Empty stomach	Presc. C Empty stomach	Presc. C Empty stomach	Presc. C Empty stomach
Bedtime	Presc. B*	Presc. B*	Presc. B*	Presc. B*	Presc. B*	Presc. B*	Presc. B*

Important: Mark the medicine with an * if you take it with food, or note other directions.

Medicine Schedule

45

Medicin

	Sunday	Monday	Tuesday
Morning			
Lunchtime			
Dinner-time			
Bedtime			

Important: Mark the medicine with an * if you take it with food,

chedule B

Wednesday	Thursday	Friday	Saturday

or note other directions.

Medicine Schedule

Medicin

	Sunday	Monday	Tuesday
Morning			
Lunchtime			
Dinner-time			
Bedtime			

Important: Mark the medicine with an * if you take it with food,

Schedule B

Wednesday	Thursday	Friday	Saturday

or note other directions.

Medical Contact Phone Book

If you are like most of us, you see more than one doctor. This information will help you, your family, and your healthcare providers to contact one another with questions or in an emergency.

Doctor	Specialty
Phone No.	Contact Name
Address	

Doctor	Specialty
Phone No.	Contact Name
Address	

Doctor	Specialty
Phone No.	Contact Name
Address	

Doctor	Specialty
Phone No.	Contact Name
Address	

Doctor	Specialty
Phone No.	Contact Name
Address	

Doctor	Specialty
Phone No.	Contact Name
Address	

Doctor	Specialty
Phone No.	Contact Name
Address	

Tracking Your Medicine

Doctor	Specialty	Contact Name
Phone No.		
Address		

Doctor	Specialty	Contact Name
Phone No.		
Address		

Practitioner	Specialty	Contact Name
Phone No.		
Address		

Dentist	Specialty	Contact Name
Phone No.		
Address		

Therapist	Specialty
Phone No.	Contact Name
Address	

Pharmacy	Pharmacist's Name
Phone No.	
Address	

Pharmacy	Pharmacist's Name
Phone No.	
Address	

V.A. Pharmacy	Pharmacist's Name
Phone No.	
Address	

Emergency Contacts

Family Member	Neighbor
Phone No.	Phone No.
Address	Address

Family Member	Neighbor
Phone No.	Phone No.
Address	Address

Family Member	Neighbor
Phone No.	Phone No.
Address	Address

Family Member	Neighbor
Phone No.	Phone No.
Address	Address

Resources

VIAL OF LIFE is a free, nationally recognized program which saves lives by providing local 911 personnel with your vital medical information when they come to your residence in an emergency. Forms and directions for Vial of Life use are available by calling your local police or fire department. Or use the Web and go to the site at *www.homeindulgences.com/vialoflife.htm* for easy instructions and a free form and identification stickers to print out, or go to *www.VialofLife.com* for instructions and a form to complete on-line or print out. It is so easy and can save your life!

WWW.GETTINGWELL.COM is the *Physician's Desk Reference* on-line with detailed information on health topics as well as drug information for prescription, over- the-counter, and natural medicines.

WWW.MEDLINEPLUS.ORG is the National Library of Medicine and National Institutes of Health in-depth guide to health and medical information, as well as prescription and over-the-counter medication information. They recently added a section specifically for older adults.

WWW.HELPINGPATIENTS.ORG provides contact information and guidelines for the 48 member drug companies and their discount programs.

WWW.TOGETHERX.COM is a site for qualified Medicare enrollees with no prescription drug coverage. It has information and applications for a drug discount card for outpatient prescription medicines from the participating pharmaceutical companies.

WWW.NCSL.ORG/PROGRAMS/HEALTH/DRUGAID.HTM offers information on state drug assistance programs.

Note: Web addresses change frequently. Check our web site, www. BoomerView.com for updates and current web resources.

34 Vital Tips For Safe Medicine Use

At The Doctor

1. Make sure any new prescription will work safely with other medicines you are taking, including supplements, herbal and homeopathic remedies, and over-the-counter medications. Tell your doctor about social drugs you use such as alcohol. Ask if this medication is safe for *you*.

2. Ask if there is written, large print patient information available about the new medicine or other medicines you have questions about. Make sure you understand the information. If you are uncertain, ask your doctor, health practitioner, or pharmacist for further explanations.

3. When you get a new prescription, ask if it is the smallest dose that will do the job.

4. Ask if there are any tests required while you are taking this medicine or when it's finished.

5. Make sure you ask about directions such as:
   ▶ Does "four times a day" mean take with meals and at bedtime; or take at 8 A.M., NOON, 4 P.M. and 8 P.M.; or take every six hours around the clock?

   ▶ When the instructions say "before meals" or "after meals," *how long* before or after meals does that mean? Can the medicine be taken with meals if that is the easiest or most convenient?

   ▶ Sometimes the directions say "take as needed." How often can "as needed" medicine be taken? How do you know "as needed" is now? How much can you take in a day?

6. If you take a prescription drug that you think works and your doctor changes it, *ask why*!

7. If you are about to get a new medicine, ask for a drug manufacturer's sample, a trial size, or a shorter prescription (7-10 days) and a refill to make up the full order. That way you don't pay for the whole course until you know there are no side effects and the medicine is working for you. However, there may be an additional pharmacy charge to fill the prescription twice, so ask.

8. Ask if there are things you should avoid doing while taking your prescriptions, such as avoiding the sun or alcohol or driving.

9. Ask if there are other things you can do to get better faster such as changing your diet, exercising, getting more or less sleep, or meditating.

10. If it isn't possible to fill out the forms at home by yourself, put all your medicine containers in a bag and make an appointment to take the whole bag to your doctor's office. Put in everything you currently take, including all of your medicines, vitamins, herbal and homeopathic supplements, and over-the-counter medicines (antacids, eye drops, pain relievers, and cold medicines). You can also ask for help filling in the PillTracker Form, Medicine List and Schedule.

At The Pharmacy

11. When you pick up your medicines at the pharmacy, ask and look to make sure you are getting the medicine, dosage, and number of pills prescribed by your doctor for your current, specific illness.

12. Ask for easy-to-open tops for your bottles if you have no children or grandchildren at home. If children visit, make sure all medicines are well out of their reach.

13. If you are given liquid medications, make sure a proper measuring device is included.

Tips

14. Most pills should not be crushed or cut because they are designed to be long-acting or to protect your stomach. Ask the pharmacist what to do if you need to crush, cut, or chew your pills or tablets.

15. If the information on the bottles is hard to read, ask for large print labels.

16. If you are given a patch, ask how often to change it and where to apply it on your body. Remember to remove the old patch before you put on a new one. If your skin becomes irritated or the patch won't stick, ask the pharmacist for assistance right away so delivery of the medication is not delayed or interrupted.

Key Safety Principles

17. Refill your prescriptions before they run out.

18. **Do not** share your medicines with others or take other people's medicines!

19. **Do not** take a larger or smaller amount of a medication than is prescribed by the doctor or is recommended on the label.

20. Call your doctor or health professional *immediately* if you are having any problems with your medicines.

21. Some medicines take days or even weeks to work, and you may not notice any change for a while. Review your *Tracking Your Medicine Guide* information, the printed information that came with the medicine, then call your doctor, health practitioner, or pharmacist if you have questions or concerns.

22. Don't stop taking a prescription medicine without talking to your doctor or other health professional, even if you "feel better" or you think it may not be working. Complete the prescription as instructed, or call the doctor and ask if you can stop.

23. Some drugs with different names contain similar ingredients and do the same thing. Check to make sure you don't "double up."

24. If you sometimes forget to take your medicines, try putting your morning pills near your cereal, lunch pills near the bread, dinner or evening pills near your TV table or phone. *Do not* put pills near your bed. You may take the wrong thing in the dark or when you are sleepy.

25. If remembering to take pills on time is difficult, think about getting a watch or pillbox with an alarm to alert you of pill-taking times.

26. If you take a chewable tablet and have dentures or bridgework, be sure to rinse your mouth well afterwards so your gums don't get irritated.

27. If the instructions are to cut your pills in half, make sure you get a special pill cutter. Using a knife may break the pills unevenly, causing the dose to be incorrect.

Storage

28. Keep all medicines in a cool, dry place. The bathroom medicine cabinet may not be the best place to store medicines. Ask if the medicine should be refrigerated or kept in a dark place.

29. If you use a divided pillbox or a pill-case, make sure the proper number of pills is included and the compartments are empty each day. Keep a sample of each pill in its original container.

30. Check the dates on your prescriptions and over-the-counter medicines. Throw expired medicines in the trash.

Tips

Keeping Costs Down

31. Ask if there is a generic equivalent for your prescription, which often costs less.

32. Ask if a higher dose pill might cost less and if it safely can be cut in half.

33. Ask for a long-term supply of a pill you take regularly, as more may be cheaper. Make sure you know how long and under what storage conditions it will remain effective.

One More Thing

34. Be smart and aware when purchasing drugs on the Internet. Check to see if your source has FDA approval or if there are guarantees that your prescriptions are correct. Watch for expired, contaminated, or incorrect doses when purchasing your medicines from outside the United States. At *www.nabp.net,* you can find Verified Internet Pharmacies that are certified by the National Association of Boards of Pharmacy.

Acknowledgments

The **BoomerView** *ElderCare Guide Series* was born after years of listening to family stories about the challenges of aging and then experiencing many of those situations personally. Adult children and partners shared their experiences with medications, hospitals, rehab centers, altering residences or moving, and, finally, hospice. I hope this first Guide will help your story to be a happy and healthy one.

This Guide is dedicated to the memories of Melvin and Mary and to the brave struggles of Ditty and Allen and all of our young-at-heart parents who deserve the best from each of us. And to David, with love.

With grateful thanks to my family and many friends, those who shared their stories and those who supported me with a critical eye. Among them: Warren Daane; Carol Hill; C.J. Hirschfield & Doug McKechnie; Barbara & Marty Kaplan; Cathi & Roger Kingston; Deena Love & John Stiles; Esther, Gus & Linda Niedweske; Fred & Nancy Ostrander; Loren Partridge; Betty & John Reilly; Jim Ross; Dr. Eric Shapira; Roberta Silverstein & Dr. Steven Sperber; Marnie Stern; Peg Symonik & Steve Zien.

Particular thanks go to my generous editor/contributors: Ron Finley of the University of California School of Pharmacy, Dr. Moira Fordyce of Stanford University, and Carol Ross of the University of Wisconsin–Milwaukee.

Laurel Zien, M.A., is a consultant in senior housing, a mediator, and family caregiver. She is a member of the American Society on Aging and a speaker on family caregiving issues.

Notes

Notes

_____

_____

_____

_____

_____

_____

_____

_____

_____

_____

_____

_____

_____

_____

_____

_____

We hope you found *Tracking Your Medicine: How to Keep It Simple and Safe* helpful, interesting, and easy to use. We would appreciate hearing your comments on this Guide for later editions, as well as your suggestions for new guides! You can e-mail us at: comments@BoomerView.com.

THANKS!

Don't forget to visit our Web site for updates, news, and discussions at www.BoomerView.com.

Order Form

Check our Web site or use this form:

Please send me:

_____ copies of *Tracking Your Medicine* for $8.95 each. $ _____

_____ Family 4-Packs for $30.45 each (15% off). $ _____

Include $3.50 for shipping and handling for one book,
and $.50 for each additional book. $ _____

For Priority Mail, add an additional $4.00 for up to six books. $ _____

California residents must include 8.25% sales tax. $ _____

Payment must accompany orders. Allow up to three weeks for delivery.
Total and enclose your check for $ _____

Name _____

Organization _____

Address _____

City/State/Zip _____

Phone_____

E-mail_____

Make your check payable and return to

BoomerView Press
3020 El Cerrito Plaza #376
El Cerrito, CA 94530

Please do not send cash. Quantity discounts available.
Prices subject to change.

www.BoomerView.com
email: sales@BoomerView.com